GRIT

How to Get a Job and Build a Career with a Criminal Record

Written by

Harley T. Blakeman

Ordering Information:

Special discounts are available on quantity purchases. For details, contact me directly at harley@honestjobs.com.

Cover Art by: Fredrick Bowman

ISBN: 978-0692848678

First Edition

Printed in the United States of America

Contents

Chapter 1: **Introduction**

Recidivism refers to a person's relapse into criminal behavior and often after incarceration or intervention for a previous crime. The Bureau of Justice Statistics performed a 5-year study, tracking a sample of inmates from 30 states following their release in 2015. Below are a few of the statistics directly from their report.

- About two-thirds (67.8%) of released prisoners were arrested for a new crime within 3 years, and three-quarters (76.6%) were arrested within 5 years.
- More than a third (36.8%) of all prisoners who were arrested within 5 years of release were arrested within the first 6 months after release, with more than half (56.7%) arrested by the end of the first year.
- Within 5 years of release, 84.1% of inmates who were age 24 or younger at release were arrested, compared to 78.6% of inmates ages 25 to 39 and 69.2% of those age 40 or older.

Although there are hundreds of pre-release programs, re-entry programs, and nonprofit organizations across the country working to reduce recidivism, ex-offenders are still having an incredibly hard time finding the positive reinforcement they need. The social stigma around people with criminal records often make it more difficult to have a smooth transition back into the community. The same stigma, along with several other issues discussed in this book, are weighing down their chances of getting a job and building a career.

Over the past 10 years, I went from being a convicted felon with nothing to being a productive citizen with a supportive community, earning a bachelor's degree in business administration, and launched my career as an operations manager. In 2019, I started my own business (www.HonestJobs.com) which is now the nation's largest fair-chance/second-chance employment platform. While your story and circumstances are likely different from my own, you will face many of the same challenges I faced along my journey. This book will provide a greater chance to break the statistics stacked against you by providing a universal set of tools and techniques that you can begin to apply right away.

Chapter 2: **My Criminal Record**

I was born in Dallas, Fort Worth, TX in 1991. My father, Douglas Blakeman, was born in Springfield, OH and my mother, Michelle Blakeman, in Texarkana, TX. My mother had a son prior to meeting my father. His name is Gregory Banister, my older brother. The four of us made up my family; aside from distant relatives, we would visit on rare occasions in Ohio and Arkansas. My father attended college in Florida at Jacksonville University but never graduated and my mother dropped out of high school to raise my older brother Greg.

Prior to my conception, my father had many job titles. At one point in his life, he was the owner of multiple Domino's Pizza stores. At another point, he owned a big rig and traveled to 48 out of 50 states. While living in Dallas, I remember that my parents ran a small company called Best Buy Moooving. This was a home and office moving company where all the trucks and trailers were painted white with black spots. I have blurry images in my head of our front yard and us celebrating Christmas in our Dallas home.

My mother received a call at our Dallas home from her mother in Hope, AR. when I was four years old. My grandfather had passed away in the night from a heart attack at 50 years of age. My grandmother had no other family living in Arkansas so there was pressure on my parents that ultimately led to us moving to help her with the house and to get through the tough times. Both of my parents had to start over from scratch with a new home, new jobs and new friends. I recall moving in with my grandma and being amazed by how huge her backyard was but slightly scared of the hundreds of Betty Boop knick-knacks she had on the walls.

Both of my parents found jobs working for a steel company called SMI Joist. My father started off as a welder and my mother worked as a secretary. Over the few years that we lived in Arkansas, my father was promoted several times and another loving man came into my grandmother's life. The timing was perfect when SMI Joist promoted my father to the engineering department and asked us to move to Florida for his new position. At eight years old I moved with my family to the small town of Keystone Heights, Florida.

Although I had a rough upbringing, I had a normal childhood up until my mid-teenage years. Most of my childhood memories are from the time I lived in Florida. In fourth grade, I made several friends whom I would stay very close with for the next ten years. The one passion my friends and I shared was skateboarding. Almost every weekend, my parents would take us to a different skate park or the beach to surf. All my friends loved hanging out at our house and thought that I had the coolest parents.

For many years, my mother had been overweight until she lost over 50 pounds on the Atkins diet. With newly found confidence, my mother started going out with new friends that my father had never met before. Needless to say, they started arguing frequently until my mother stopped coming home on the weekends. I honestly didn't understand the implications of my parents separating until my mother told my brother and me that she was pregnant with another man's baby. The divorce followed quickly after that. Although my mother did a poor job of staying in our lives, my father stayed remarkably strong and took care of my brother and me on his own.

Less than one year later, I was called out of my eighth-grade math class to find my older brother and the principle waiting for me in the hallway. The news was crushing when I heard that my father was in critical condition at Shands Hospital in Gainesville, Florida. On the ride to the hospital, my older brother explained that all he knew was that my father was involved in an accident while driving his motorcycle to work, and that it was bad. When we arrived at the hospital, a doctor took my brother and me to a room and explained that my father was on life support which was keeping his heart beating but that he was brain-dead due to severe head trauma. The doctor said it's believed that people in this condition can still hear family and advised us to go into the room, express our love and say our goodbyes. Truthfully, I wish I hadn't seen my father in that condition.

Drugs were never a problem for my brother and me before our father passed. I had tried beer and smoked marijuana once or twice but that was just kids being kids. In the late 2000s, the state of Florida was a huge source for prescription pills which contributed to a national opioid epidemic. I don't have the numbers, but a lot of teenagers and their parents were abusing painkillers. Between my mother leaving and my father passing away, my brother and I were dealing with pretty severe anxiety and depression. In my hometown, it was easy for us to find Xanax, a highly addictive yet effective anti-anxiety prescription pill. The problem was that these drugs simply postponed, and usually compounded the negative effects. Once I had started taking non-prescribed Xanax, I soon got comfortable taking OxyContin and doing cocaine which caused greater insecurity and depression.

It would be unfair not to mention my mother's attempts at parenting. Shortly after my father's funeral, my mother invited me to meet the father of my little brother so that I could stay with them. I gave it a try for a while but was never very comfortable with the situation. A few weeks after meeting this man, my mother told me that they were going to have another child and that he just got a great job offer in Savannah, Georgia. I contemplated staying in Florida with my older brother but didn't have a car or job to support myself at fifteen years old.

Once we settled into Pooler, a suburb of Savannah, things actually started looking up for us. I made some good friends at Westgate High School that I would go skateboarding with nearly every day. Although my new friends and I drank and smoked weed, we were decent kids. Shortly after the move, I was able to buy myself a new car with my father's life insurance and started my first job at a local Sonics. We had only lived in Savannah for a month when my mother's new husband was fired from his new job. Three months later, he was still unemployed and we were moving back to Florida.

Moving back to Florida was rough because we moved into a tiny trailer where I didn't even have my own bedroom. The trailer was also about twenty minutes away from my brother and all my friends. Most nights, I stayed with friends because it was more convenient and less awkward. Moving back was also the beginning of the end for my mom and her husband. My attendance and grades were suffering due to my living situation as well as my new drug habit. Not long after restarting school in Florida, the principal pulled me aside and asked that I consider getting my GED instead of trying to finish high school because I was missing class so often. He also said that the administration was aware of my drug addiction and thought I was jeopardizing other students.

Dropping out of high school made sense at the time. I was failing classes and didn't have clean clothes most of the time. I was homeless, by definition, and badly addicted to painkillers. What started as selling weed in high school, quickly led to selling harder drugs as a dropout. Shortly after dropping out of high school, one of my friends from Savannah came to Florida to visit me. While he was in town, he discovered that I had access to cheap prescription pills, specifically Roxicodone. He explained that people in Savannah pay three times what I was paying in Florida and that they were also hard to find there. I fully understood the risk I was taking, but I felt as if I had nothing to lose and everything to gain.

The next week, I visited my friend in Savannah and brought thirty-five Roxys (Roxicodone) with me. It was less than 4 hours that I was in town before I had sold all thirty-five for a profit of roughly $500. At seventeen years old, I thought I had discovered a gold mine. My friend knew a dozen or so people who all wanted to buy more and in larger quantities. Two weeks later, I visited Savannah again with a hundred pills and made well over $1,000 profit. My relationships with the supplier and clientele grew rapidly until I was selling hundreds of Roxy's and Xanax, making thousands of dollars every week. My friend and I decided to get an apartment together in Savannah, where we operated our business.

After a few months of making my weekly trips between Florida and Georgia, I was arrested at a red light just a few blocks from my Savannah apartment. Chatham Narcotics Team surrounded my car and pulled me out at gunpoint. Once I was apprehended, the police asked if they could search my vehicle and I told them no, but they proceeded to search the vehicle anyway. This was the first time I was ever arrested and I had just turned eighteen years old.

For the purpose of this book, there is no need for me to go into all the details of the arrest. I was charged with multiple felonies, including intent to distribute marijuana, Xanax, Roxicodone, and Valium, then released on bail after two days in the Chatham County Jail. The police seized the drugs, my car, and all my cash. I was left with nothing but a drug addiction and a court date set eleven months out.

While I was out on bond, my life seemed to only get worse. I lost my job and my girlfriend. She was no longer interested in me after she found out I was not getting back my money or vehicle. I was taking excessive amounts of Xanax in an attempt to cope with the situation and anyone who has wrestled with Xanax knows it makes you do incredibly dumb things. I was arrested a second time for shoplifting a pair of Polo pants in the Savannah mall with the plan of reselling them for $50. It was a terrible plan. Luckily, I was able to get out on bond again for less than a hundred dollars which was paid by my roommate's mother.

After my second arrest I decided to go back to Florida. Over the next nine months leading up to my court date for the drug charges, I sold weed and made enough money to feed my own drug addiction. One night, I took a lot of Xanax and went to Walmart in Starke, Florida with a few friends. I was arrested again for walking out with a cart full of groceries. At least that is what the officers told me the next morning when I woke up dazed and confused. My one phone call was used to call the mother of one of my longtime childhood friends. His mother came and paid the one hundred dollars to get me out of jail for my third time.

A month or two later, I was at a friend's house when the Clay County police knocked on the door. They explained that they knew I had stolen a diamond ring from an old lady's house on the other side of town and that they had a warrant for my arrest. I couldn't believe what I was hearing. I told the police that I had nothing to do with the incident and asked why they thought it was me. The officer explained that a girl was arrested for stealing her own grandmother's ring, but once she was in custody, she and her significant other (who were drug addicts themselves) wrote witness statements saying that I had committed the crime. The officer said if I was truly innocent, I should turn myself in and that's what I did. After an hour or so of questioning, I was taken to jail with no evidence other than the written statements the granddaughter of the victim had provided. I was not allowed a bond this time because I was being charged with a felony while on felony bond. The ring was never.

Up until this point, I had been guilty of drug trafficking and of shoplifting, but I was not guilty of stealing this wedding ring. For the first time, I reached out to my father's side of the family in Ohio for help. I explained my innocence and my aunt offered to hire a cheap attorney to help me fight the felony theft charge. I was facing serious time in Georgia, where they requested that I be sent to them once I had served my sentence in Florida. This meant that I would be doing hard time, right away, regardless of the outcome of the theft case. I met with the attorney only one time and that was right before my first court hearing. He asked me a lot of questions but didn't seem to believe that I was innocent. All his questions were about my past charges, drug habits, and my lack of parents. After he was finished talking to me, he left the room for twenty minutes or so.

When he returned, he explained to me my options, "You can fight this case but you will have to stay here for several more months before going to Georgia to serve your time there, or you could plead no contest to the theft charge. The D.A. has agreed to give you time served with no probation. If you did this, you could start serving time in Georgia now and get out a lot earlier. I also believe that because you're only eighteen and you've technically never been convicted of anything before, the judge will probably withhold the felony from your permanent record." He also said he wasn't telling me what to do, but that with the charges in Georgia over my head, I was going to be a felon

14

anyway. My aunt hired the attorney to work in my best interest so I did what he was clearly suggesting and pled "no contest" under the condition that the judge consider withholding the felony from my record. The judge denied our request and sent me on my way with my first felony conviction. It's the one crime I didn't commit, and the only crime that stills shows up on my criminal record today.

Around 9:45pm that night, my name was called over the intercom of the dorm room I was living in. "Harley Blakeman, pack it up. You're going to Georgia". Adrenaline ran through my body as the officers briefed me on the transportation process. They explained that I would be riding in the back of a van with some other prisoners as they put shackles on my hands and feet. Before I could even understand what had just occurred, I was being extradited to Georgia for another court case, this time without an attorney.

My public defender in Georgia actually did a pretty good job. The D.A. was requesting that I be sentenced to three years in prison, but she was able to get my sentence down to one year, not counting the time I had already served. Granted, I would also have to do four hundred hours of community service with ten years of probation. It sounds bad, but I would rather not be in prison any longer than I absolutely had to be.

There is no upside to prison. It was terrible. However, I feel like I made the most of the situation. I read dozens of books, earned my G.E.D., and was sober for the first time in years. Prison also led to me building a relationship with my father's family, namely my grandmother and my twin aunts. We would write each other letters weekly and they would send me photos and update me on their lives. As my release date got closer, one of my aunts told me that if I wanted to move to Columbus, Ohio, I could stay in her basement for a month or so until I got back on my feet. A feeling of hope was reintroduced to me at that time - just having someone care about my well-being and my future changed everything.

My aunt and my grandmother drove from Ohio to Georgia the morning of March 12, 2012 to pick me up on my release date. I had no plan as to what I would do in the new city other than try and stay out of trouble. My aunts knew a family that owned a few restaurants in town and helped me get an interview. I was offered a job working in their kitchen making $8.25/hour. My aunt and uncle had a short set of rules I had to follow while I was living with them that helped me build good daily habits and set priorities. Although I only lived with them for two months, their influence on me has been key to my ongoing success.

Now fast-forward ten and a half years. I started with a prison G.E.D. and went on to graduate from The Ohio State University with honors. I started working in fast food and went on to land a great job before becoming an Entrepreneur. The best part is that I was able to accomplish this while being open and honest about my felony convictions.

I understand that your story and situation will be different from mine. Not everyone will have someone give them a place to stay or help them find their first job, and not everyone will want or need to go to college to have a successful career. Regardless, you will need to know how to set yourself apart from the crowd, explain your criminal record, and grow your career. The next nine chapters of this book explain how you can change your life forever by getting a job and building your career with a criminal record.

Chapter 3: **Survival Check List**

This chapter is very brief as to not waste your time with fairly straightforward issues. Before jumping into the job market, it would be wise to review this survival checklist. You may have already taken care of some, if not all, of these issues. Or you may have to spend the next month or two working them out as I did. Below is a list of things that are critical to finding and maintaining any type of decent employment.

- ☐ Clothes, Shoes, Umbrella & Jacket
- ☐ Social security card & state ID
- ☐ Address you can use for mail
- ☐ Reliable transportation (Bus Pass, Bicycle, Car, etc.)
- ☐ Access to a computer and internet (Library)
- ☐ Email (Gmail is free!)
- ☐ Cell phone
- ☐ Checking account
- ☐ Identified support system (Family, A.A., Church, etc.)
- ☐ Finish reading this book

You should work your way down this list and try to gain access to or ownership of these resources. If you can check all of these items off, then you are in business.

Some of the items will be harder to obtain than others, such as a social security card or cell phone, so it is important that you ask for help where you need it. Show this checklist to someone from your identified support system and let them know where you could use some help. Anyone who is willing to help you out with your checklist may be willing to help you with other things covered later in this book. Thank them for their help and be sure to stay in contact.

You should not postpone your job search until you have checked off the entire list but rather work towards completing the list while looking for employment. Look for cheap clothes, transportation, and cell phones to hold you over for the next 6-12 months. I didn't have a cell phone for the first 8 weeks I was employed and didn't have a car for nearly a year. I rode an old hand-me-down 12-speed bike to work until I bought a 1992 Acura on Craigslist for $1,000.

Think of what you need to do to check off each item on the list. Make a to-do list with names of people you need to talk to and places you need to visit. This can be a stressful and trying process, so be patient and stay positive. You will have the checklist completed sooner than you may think if you stay focused.

If you haven't already done so, I recommend creating an account with www.honestjobs.com to access our national resource center. Using this free tool, you can find local non-profits and agencies that can help you with most of your critical needs.

Chapter 4: **Are You Ready?**

The fact of the matter is that you and I are currently at a disadvantage in the job market. Most other applicants are going to check "No" next to the question - "Have you ever been convicted of a crime?" The frustration of giving it your best effort and constantly being rejected, application after application, can become overwhelming quickly, but there is more to the problem than just failing a background check. Most people with criminal records come from troubled homes or lifestyles. Your past probably caused you to pick up some bad habits and neglect your better ones. The environment or punishment you may have gone through could have also impacted your of way thinking. To build something that will last, you must first lay a solid foundation. Your mindset is absolutely critical to having a strong foundation.

Mindset

First, I think it is important to address a few facts.

1.) It doesn't matter if you were guilty or innocent.

2.) You have a criminal record.

3.) You have to accept it and move forward.

Having a victim mentality will always stop you from getting ahead in life.

I was arrested and convicted of a crime I didn't commit in Florida at 19 years old. At first, I held resentment against the people who claimed I committed the crime and even more so against the courts that pressured me into pleading "no contest". Eventually, I realized that this happened to me because I was living wrong. Although I didn't commit the crime, I was using drugs and hanging out with the wrong crowd. This type of thing doesn't usually happen to people who stay clean and surround themselves with good people.

1.) Don't blame others for your criminal record.

2.) Don't use your criminal record as an excuse.

No one likes a person who blames others for their circumstances. Take ownership and throw out the victim mentality!

Once you've decided to abandon the victim mindset forever, the best tool you can pick up is a determined mindset. Vince Lombardi observed, "Winning isn't everything, but wanting to win is". The four-time Olympic gold medalist, Jesse Owens, proclaimed, "The battles that count aren't the ones for gold medals. The struggles within yourself – The invisible, inevitable battles inside all of us- that's where it's at." The voice and thoughts in your own head can tear you down or they can build you up.

Don't let anyone, including yourself, tell you there is something you can't do. No one can stop a person who will stop for no one. Go back to college, start that business, write a book; You are in control of your own destiny. The key to turning a determined mindset into successful achievement lies in setting goals. Nearly all great things begin with a goal.

Once you decide what goal you want to achieve, commit to it. Try and set goals that are **S.M.A.R.T.** (Specific, Measurable, Attainable, Realistic and Time-bound). For instance, let's say you want to make some extra money selling used books. Your S.M.A.R.T. goal might read something like this:

Specific: I will sell used business books on Amazon.com.

Measurable: I will buy 20 used business books by next Sunday, and I will aim to sell a minimum of five per week.

Attainable: I will get set up on Amazon first. Then, I will build an inventory of 50 used business books to sell. I will write every customer a thank you note to gain repeat customers.

Relevant: While I am waiting for books to sell, I can read them, gaining business knowledge to expand my business.

Time-Based: My Amazon account will be up and running with books for sale within four days.

Write your S.M.A.R.T. goal down with a list of short-term steps to help you succeed and check them off as you go. Put your list in a visible place so you can reflect on it daily for motivation. When the famous Les Brown talked about overcoming tough circumstances, he said, "You must have patience and engage in consistent action." Building the life you want for yourself isn't easy, but if you set goals and follow Mr. Brown's advice, it can be done. Have dreams big enough to scare you, set goals that are challenging yet achievable, and consistently take steps towards your goals.

Studies show a strong correlation between inmates and successful entrepreneurs when looking at work habits such as perseverance, adaptability, and GRIT. Incarceration teaches you to get comfortable with things moving slowly (days). As an entrepreneur, it takes years to build a successful business and as an employee, it takes years to build a successful career. Patience and resilience are key to reaching your goals as well as getting a job and building your career.

Your Habits

The higher the position you're applying for, the tougher the interview process will be. Some jobs have a very simple hiring process. In an interview I had with Champs, a sports restaurant in Columbus, Ohio, I explained that I was a fast learner, dependable, and hardworking. They simply trusted me and asked when I could start.

However, interviews for higher-level positions, such as District Manager for Aldi or Sales Manager for Cintas, were a whole different story. Usually, these positions involve several rounds of interviews, saturated with behavioral-based questions. After asking a few of these questions, hiring managers will be able to tell if you have good or bad daily habits. Therefore, it is critical that you evaluate and adjust your habits before applying for a job; the sooner, the better!

There are many types of good and bad habits that I could write about, but I have chosen to focus on the ones most important to successfully getting a job and building a career. Most successful people would agree that massive success isn't reached by the big things you do, but rather by the little things done consistently that make up your daily habits. Research indicates that on average it takes 66 days to form a new habit. Although, the number of days can vary depending on the behavior, the person, and the circumstances. Your goal should be to embrace the process and before you know, it you will have formed the habits you want. If you want to lose weight, exercise daily. If you want to learn a second language, practice daily. If you want to successfully land a job and build your career, you'll need to develop the type of daily habits hiring managers are looking for.

Spend Your Time Wisely

One way to address your daily habits is to think about how you spend your time. Whether you are currently searching for a job or just hoping to grow your current career, your time is a valuable resource that should be used efficiently. When I was incarcerated, an old man told me to try and stay busy because, "An idle mind is the devil's playground." If you want to stay out of trouble, stay busy. If you want to get a job and build a career, stay busy doing things that add value to you as an employee.

If you've just gotten out, or you are soon to be released, it is important that you fill your time with work as quickly as possible. Your family and friends will understand that you are often busy with work and will respect it. Try not to be too picky while searching for your first job. This job is only meant to bring in *some* income and to keep you busy while you look for a better job that will give you more responsibility and/or better pay. It's never good to overwork yourself, but the plus side of working a lot is that you will be able to save some money and it will give you more experience to talk about in your next interview.

Depending on the specification of your sentencing, you may have an intimidating amount of community service you must complete before a certain deadline. Do not procrastinate getting this started. Use this simple equation to determine the minimum hours you should volunteer per week. (Total weeks – 12 weeks) / (# of community service hours). You want to subtract at least 12 weeks from the total available time to complete your community service to account for any unexpected events. For example, when I was released, I had two years (112 weeks) to complete a staggering 400 hours of community service.

112 weeks – 12 weeks = 100 weeks

400 hours ÷ 100 weeks = 4 hours a week

There are endless ways you could spend your free time. Watching TV, scrolling the internet, and playing video games aren't bad things if you can do them in moderation. However, you should make it a habit to read something daily. Setting aside time every day to read the newspaper or a chapter of a book is very beneficial. I enjoy books on business, entrepreneurship, and leadership.

Not everyone will know what they are passionate about or what career they want to pursue. If you're not sure, spend some of your free time studying different career paths now. Search the internet for "Free Career Quiz" and see what you get. These tests take into consideration your education, skills, and personality. If you do know where you want to take your career, start studying more in-depth materials. Learn as much as you can about the industry, the company, and the position. Read books or watch YouTube tutorials on the technical and soft skills required for the line of work you are interested in. Whether it is to start your own business or become a college professor, studying the subject will accelerate your success.

From engineers to entrepreneurs to politicians, the single most important key to success is networking and getting to know people! The importance of networking is tenfold for people with criminal records. It's also a great way to find out what careers are most interesting to you. Later in the book, I go into more depth on the topic, but for now, I will say it's one of the best habits to pick up. Have a genuine interest in other people, especially people you are meeting for the first time. Make it a habit to remember people's names and say their names every time you see them. This is a sure way to make a great impression and build your network.

Unemployment Habits

There's a core set of qualities that you must have just to get/keep a job. These include:

1.) Good hygiene is a must (Shower, use deodorant, and brush your teeth daily)
2.) Punctuality (Be the person who always shows up five minutes early)
3.) Use good manners (To customers, coworkers and your boss)

These are habits that you have probably already mastered but if you haven't, get on it now! Failing to master these three habits is a sure-fire way to stay unemployed or get fired.

The fact that you are reading this book means that you are ready to start building a career. To be successful on this journey, you may want to clean up your past a little.

For me this meant deactivating my old Myspace and Facebook accounts that had pictures I wouldn't want employers to see. In this day and age anyone can find your information online. If you wouldn't want to show it to the person who may be interviewing you, then remove it from the internet. Avoid putting any pictures or thoughts online unless they are a good representation of the person you would want a prospective employer to see.

The last group of habits addressed in this chapter are huge. Drugs, alcohol, and reckless behavior will keep you from building your career, and likely, from getting a job in the first place. Not to mention, many of the people reading this book, like myself, are on some form of probation. It may be possible to use drugs and alcohol without violating probation and perhaps even hold down a job. If you choose to take that risk, never do it before going to work. I can promise you that you're not going to move up very far in the company you're working for if you continue with bad habits. The old you wasted time on mindless fun but the new you is on a mission to better your life. The new you wants to achieve your goals more than just the short-term satisfaction that drugs and alcohol provided in the past.

Unless you are Floyd "Money" Mayweather or The Notorious Connor McGregor, talking tough and knocking people's lights out won't make you a millionaire. In fact, it will more than likely cause you to lose the few great opportunities that are around you. I fully understand the importance of this behavior while you are incarcerated. However, getting a job and building a career with a criminal record is a whole different ball game. You will need to learn to bite your tongue when you want to cuss a coworker out. When your "not so hard-working" boss tells you to stop standing around and go clean the bathrooms, you'll need to swallow your pride, smile, and clean the bathrooms. If nothing else, building the habit of staying cool and friendly in times of conflict proves that you are a well-tempered employee and fit for a managerial position.

Daily habits repeated consistently are what create great success. There is a famous quote that says, "Many things aren't equal but everyone gets the same 24 hours a day, 7 days a week. We make time for what we truly want." You can watch TV or you can read Dale Carnegie's book, "How to Win Friends and Influence People". You can go kick it with Craig on Friday or you can work that double shift and make some money to start your business. At the end of the day, you are in control of your own life. The jobs you get, the salary you earn, and the respect people show you are determined by your actions. Take responsibility for your daily actions and turn them into good and productive habits.

Chapter 5: **Preparing for the Job Search**

Fisher College of Business at The Ohio State University puts a lot of effort into preparing students for their job search. From creating the perfect resume and elevator pitch, to researching companies and interviewing. I learned a great deal about the job search during my time at Fisher and it has paid off. The one thing business school couldn't help me with was learning how to handle all these challenging situations with a felony on my record. I learned how to deal with my unique situation through years of trial and error. In this chapter, I share with you the best way to prepare for your job search with a criminal record.

Know Yourself

Believe it or not, simply knowing yourself is the most important part of the job search. One of the most commonly asked interview questions is, "Why do you want this job?" followed up by, "What are your strengths and weaknesses?" or "Where do you see yourself in five years?" Do yourself a huge favor and get to know yourself well enough to answer these questions with confidence.

You should know your strengths, weaknesses, and what you are passionate about. Knowing yourself is very beneficial as it helps you set meaningful goals in life and in your career. It also shows that you make informed decisions with the big picture in mind, which is an extremely valuable trait in the eyes of an employer. Not having a clear understanding of who you are as an individual or as an employee is step one to a disappointing interview.

Make an honest effort to learn about yourself through introspection and by soliciting feedback from others. It can be hard to hear others tell you about your weaknesses. However, asking your co-workers and managers for feedback on your performance will accelerate the learning curve and show that you are eager to grow in the company. It's said that focusing on your strengths is the best way to reach your full potential, rather than worrying about your weaknesses. A great resource for learning and developing your strengths is a little book titled, "Strength Finder 2.0" by Tom Rath.

What Do You Love?

Discovering what you're passionate about is not an easy task for most people, but everyone should work towards finding it. Being passionate about something helps keep you happy and healthy by bringing you a sense of purpose. Your passion could be sports, religion, social work, fashion, teaching, or any other topic. Personally, my passions are fishing, reading, and helping people overcome their criminal records. Consider ways that you can tie your hobby or passion to some sort of social cause such as running a half marathon to raise money for cancer, or working a food drive at your local church. Having hobbies or a passion gives you character and good employers will value your character just as much as your technical skills.

Below is a graphic that I first saw during a leadership class. The professor asked each student to take a few minutes to think about the graphic and write a paragraph explaining what jobs or careers might be in the shaded triangle for each of us.

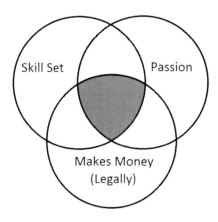

Figure 1. The Gray Area

Think about this graphic for a moment and write about what jobs and careers would allow you to be in the shaded triangle, seen in Figure 1. This exercise is how I came up with the idea to start Honest Jobs – the free online employment service that helps formerly incarcerated people connect with over 1,200 fair-chance employers.

Know the Company

Companies want to hire people who love and care about them and their brand. Hiring managers can easily tell the difference in someone who is here to interview with company "X" and someone who is excited to finally be interviewing with "THE X company" – leader in North

American manufacturing. The two subtle differences are enthusiasm and knowledge of the company. You should always know the company you are interviewing with inside and out, and at least be good at acting enthusiastic.

Before you ever sit down for your first interview with a company, you should research them. You should have general knowledge of the industry, what the company does, and how they do it. Researching the company prepares you to answer questions they will have for you such as, "Why do you want to work here?" and "What do you think makes us better than our competitors?" It will also help you come up with some meaningful questions for you to ask them, which is equally important.

Start on the internet by Googling the name of the company and reading the content on their website. Companies often have informational videos on YouTube as well. If you know someone who already works for the company you are interviewing with, ask them if you could meet with them to talk about the company and what their job is like. Most people love to talk about themselves and will be happy to tell you about their position and the company.

What Does the Company Love?

In addition to knowing about the industry, what the company does and how they do it, you should know why. Of course, they are in business to make money but businesses are not usually successful unless they care about the problems they solve for their customers. Many companies live by their core values or their mission statement, while some firms just explain their love for the business. Home Depot's core values are "Excellent customer service. Taking care of our people. Building strong relationships. And respect for all people" and the mission statement for SpaceX is "Making Humanity Multiplanetary".

I hope that you can see how knowing this information about the companies you are interested in will help you get the job and build your career. Regardless of the industry in which you are searching, any hiring manager will be pleasantly surprised when you explain how their values and mission align with your skills and passions. You absolutely need to know your strengths, weaknesses, and passions, as well as the company you are interviewing with and their passion as a company.

Where to Apply

If you are currently unemployed, your goal should be to get any job you can. Depending on your situation, you may have a car, a bicycle, or just the shoes on your feet. You should ask yourself: "Can I get to this job every day – rain, shine or snow?" For every business that you can definitely get to, you should apply. You desperately need the income, so don't neglect your first job but know that you can always look for a better one. With a felony record, you can usually get a job in a restaurant's kitchen, washing dishes or cooking to start, until you prove yourself.

I do not believe there are specific jobs that people with criminal records should or should not apply for. You should use your personal network, skills, and salesmanship to get the job you believe you deserve. It's worth noting that in most cities there are businesses that intentionally hire people with criminal records. These are commonly referred to as fair-chance or second-chance employers.

Getting an Interview

Now that you can confidently speak about yourself and the company you want to interview with, make contact with the company and express your interest. As frustrating as online applications can be, you should search the company website and apply for any open positions before calling or walking in. If you call or walk in first, you will likely be sent to the website anyway.

Its best to wait until 48 hours after submitting your online applications before calling or walking in. This gives the managers some time to see and review your application. When you call or walk in, ask if you can speak with a hiring manager. If there is not a manager available at the time, let them know the position you are interested in and ask them when the best time to come back (or call back) would be.

The key here is perseverance. You have to take charge - filling out the online applications, following up by walking in, and calling back to check on your application status. At every point of contact, you should be respectful and express how grateful you are for their consideration.

What to Wear

You should always dress for the position you want, not the position you're currently in. People often make assumptions about others based on one obvious characteristic. Social Scientists and Human Resource professionals call this projection bias. This is to say that a hiring manager might make the projection that you are management material because you are wearing a suit instead of jeans and a polo. The last thing you want is to have your prospective employer make projections that don't play in your favor.

Ladies

For most positions you will be applying for, you should play it safe and dress conservatively. Consider wearing the following:

- Dress pants or a skirt (never higher than your knees).
- Mid or long-sleeve blouse.
- Flats or heels.

When interviewing for a more professional position, you should wear a suit, or dress pants and a blazer. An extremally successful female professional told me that she always recommends that women cover up their skin for interviews. She suggested that it was in a woman's best interest to be seen and valued for her abilities and not her appearance.

If you happen to get an interview with a company in the fashion retail industry, you may be able to dress a little more casually. These companies want to hire people that have styles consistent with their brands.

Gentlemen

No matter what position is you are applying for you should always wear the following:

- A long sleeve button-up dress shirt.
- Slacks or khakis pants.
- Dress socks and dress shoes.
- A plain belt.

You should also tuck your shirt in. For any management position or a position in a professional setting, you should wear a suit and tie as seen in Figure 2. Up until just about a year ago, I had two suits, both of which I bought at thrift stores for less than forty dollars. As long as your clothes are clean and fit you well, there is no need to spend a lot before you get the job.

Figure 2. Professional Dress

The little details can have a huge impact when it comes time for managers to decide whom they want to hire. Having a fresh haircut and a clean shave shows that you care about your appearance and that you will be a good representation of the company for which you are interviewing. Avoid wearing lots of jewelry or excessive cologne or perfume.

Do You Have a Resume?

Let's start by talking about what you should have when you show up for your interview (five minutes early). Find yourself a nice leather padfolio to hold your three resumes and your pin. These are sold at Staples, Walmart, Target and on Amazon. The padfolio should have a notepad for taking any important notes and slots for the interviewers' business cards should they offer you one. You always want to bring at least three resumes so that everyone can have a copy during the interview, including yourself. If this is a high-level position, you may want to consider printing your resumes on resume paper (also sold at the places mentioned earlier).

It's not the end of your career if your resume is out of date or if you don't have one at all. Actually, it's quite the contrary. When you set up your account with Honest Jobs, the system automatically generates a resume for you using the information you provide. See the example of my resume in Figure 3 on the next page.

Harley Blakeman

Blakeman.26@gmail.com
122 E. Houston St. Apt. 6B
Columbus, OH 43201
(614) 523-####

EDUCATION:

THE OHIO STATE UNIVERSITY   **Columbus, OH**
Bachelor of Science in Business Administration   *May 2017*
Specialization: Operations Management   *GPA: 3.6/4.0*

WORK EXPERIENCE:

ASSET STRATEGY TEAM   **Columbus, OH**
Retail Consulting: Data Clerk   *January 2016 - Present*
- Compare incoming data to current records to catch payment errors using multiple databases
- Distribute bills, invoices and recollections to the correct lease analysts when errors are found
- Input correct and post-dispute data into our databases for future reference

THE OIL STORE   **Columbus, OH**
Retail Store: Assistant Manager   *May 2015 – January 2016*
- Provide customer service and sales of perishable goods up to $2,500 daily
- Manage daily operations: open and close store, report sales, schedule store events, monitor inventory and maintain records for forecasting purposes
- Implement policies to track and improve product and packaging waste

GENJI GO   **Columbus, OH**
Japanese Restaurant: Server and Chef   *March 2012 – May 2015*
- Worked as an effective team member in high pressure situations with daily sales of $10,000+
- Continually trained new Chefs as the company opened five new locations

INVOLVEMENT & LEADERSHIP:

BUCKEYEFIT   **OHIO STATE UNIVERSITY**
Student Organization: Treasurer   *August 2014 – May 2015*
- Assist in informing and coaching biweekly meetings and Crossfit workouts
- Managing semi-annual programing funds totaling $2,000+ to support weekly operations, marketing, and social events.

FISHER LEADERS   **FISHER COLLEGE OF BUSINESS**
Invitation-Only Leadership Program   *January 2016 – Present*
- Must be in top 10% of Fisher by GPA, complete interview process and write an essay to enter
- Work with a team of current MBA students to complete a pro-bono consulting project, participate in group projects with 360 feedback, attend executive workshops and perform community service

CSCMP SCPro FUNDAMENTALS CERTIFICATIONS   **COLUMBUS STATE COMMUNITY COLLEGE**
Certificates Include: *May 2016 – August 2016*
- Supply Chain Inventory Management – Warehousing Operations Management

Figure 3. Example Resume

Chapter 6: **Explaining Your Record**

Interviewing with a criminal record is frustrating for many reasons. You want to be upfront and honest about your past situations, but you don't want to eliminate your chances of getting the position. It's also hard to tell when you should bring up your record, or if you should bring it up at all. Should you tell them on the application, at the first-round interview, or once they make you a job offer? I've been through over 100 interviews since I was released in 2012 and have tried many different approaches. This chapter focuses on IF, WHEN, and HOW to tell your potential new employer about your criminal record.

Do You Tell Them

Many employers, especially restaurants, ask you if you have ever been convicted of a crime on the application, but don't actually run the background check. You may want to say 'no' on the application and hope for the best. The upside to this is that if you do get the job, you can earn money, build your resume, and potentially learn a new skill set. However, there are many downsides to this approach.

If you're planning on interviewing for a job without telling them about your criminal record, you should ask yourself two questions:

1.) Are you ok randomly getting fired?

In most states, your employer has the right to fire you for not informing them of your criminal record, and if they find out you lied to them, that's likely what they will do. I took this risk more than once early in my career so that I could make more money and gain new skills. Luckily, they never discovered my record.

2.) Do you want a career with this company?

If you answer yes, then you have to tell them about your criminal record. Let's say you want to work for a construction company while you pursue a degree in engineering. Once you graduate, you could be promoted to a professional engineering position, but that's only if you told them the truth about your record. Most positions that require managing people, money, or expensive/dangerous equipment will require a background check, and if you are currently working for the company, a promotion will likely prompt a mandatory background check.

If you have a college education or have years of valuable industry experience, you should get comfortable discussing your record with hiring managers every time. Utilizing Chapter Four you should be able to present yourself in a way that showcases your immense value to the company. You will likely be rejected many times after being upfront and honest about your criminal record, but that's ok. This is great practice and the more you try, the greater your chances of interviewing with someone who will value your skills and your honesty.

The social stigmas around people with criminal records make it difficult to openly discuss your past mistakes without jeopardizing your chances of employment. Unfortunately, there is no one-size-fits-all approach to dealing with this issue. You may avoid telling an employer about your record once or twice, but I would suggest moving to the upfront and honest method as soon as possible. This approach takes a lot of time, effort, and resilience because you will be preparing to interview for jobs that you will likely not get. However, getting hired after being honest with the interviewer about your record is your ticket to building a solid reputation and career with the company.

Now or Later

Let's say that you've decided to be honest (best practice) about your past with the companies to which you are applying and interviewing. Some applications will ask you if you have been convicted of a crime. It will either ask *"Have you been convicted of a crime in the last **seven years**?"* while others may ask *"Have you **ever** been convicted of a crime?"* Regardless of how they ask you, being honest at this point could hurt your outcome. A manager at a major fast-food chain once told me that they throw away applications that indicate the applicant has a criminal record to help narrow down the interviewing process. This is an unfair practice that practically ruins all of your chances for employment. The good news is that over the last several years many companies have stopped asking this question on applications.

It's up to you if you want to check yes or no. If you check "no" on the application, be prepared to explain why you wanted to tell them about your criminal record in person instead of telling them on the application.

If you check "yes", be sure to have a thoughtful explanation with no spelling or grammatical errors. I recommend saving your explanation in a word document so that you can copy and paste it into applications as needed. This will save you a lot of time and energy as you apply for jobs online.

Note: If you have reason to believe the company is a "fair-chance" or "second-chance" employer, you should always tell them about your criminal record.

Don't Ask, Don't Tell

In 2015, I interviewed with a large home window manufacturer in Ohio for an Operations Intern position. A few days after my interview, I received a call and was asked if I could visit the plant (1-hour drive) for a second-round interview. Toward the end of the second round, he told me that I was the guy for the job and that I would get a formal offer via email later that week. After accepting the job offer and pay of $18 an hour, I told everyone how excited I was about the opportunity.

Two to three weeks later, I got another email saying that they regret to inform me I was no longer eligible for the position because I failed the background check. This really crushed my hopes of ever building my career. The company never asked me about my background on the application or at any point in our interviews. My thought process was; they didn't ask, so they must not care. Even though they determined that my values, skills, and personality were the best fit for the position, I was turned down after receiving an offer because I didn't tell them about my criminal record. This incident caused me stress beyond belief. I wasted money and several hours of my time on driving and preparation for the interview, all because I didn't tell them about my record upfront.

Tell Them Before They Ask

In 2016 it was my senior year of business school, and I was interviewing with several companies. I was focused on a half dozen well-known companies and had strategic plans on how to tell them about my record. The week of the college recruiting cycle I received an email from a manufacturing company that I had never heard of before, inviting me to interview with them the next week. Although I was not all that interested (probably because I didn't know the company), I agreed to the interview and started preparing.

When I walked into the interview and introduced myself to the two gentlemen, I fully expected to go over my resume and begin answering behavioral-based questions. To my surprise, the more senior gentleman said, "We've looked over your resume and have a feel for your capabilities. We'd like to just talk about your life and who you are as a person." At that moment, I decided I had nothing to lose so I told the full truth. Walking them through a timeline I explained my childhood circumstances, troubled teenage years, how I paid for my mistakes as a young adult, and lastly, everything I was doing to move on and create a better life for myself. Without a word, one of them stood up, shook my hand, and said, "I'd like to hire you".

Through all my experience interviewing with a felony on my record, I have learned that being upfront and honest is the best practice. If they decide that your record makes you ineligible for the position, at least you are no longer wasting your time and energy pursuing a fruitless route. Additionally, most people will appreciate your honesty and the fact that you are working hard to overcome your past mistakes. You never know, the person who is interviewing you may have a brother, sister, mom, or dad in prison right now. Perhaps they may have even done some time themselves!

Net Positive

The secret to explaining your criminal record is to tell a strong and compelling story. Your story will have pluses and minuses but it should end with a net positive. Be upfront and honest but only talk about the things that are relevant. Make sure that you end on a good note, explaining the valuable lessons you have learned because of your situation and how it has made you a better person.

Start by thanking your interviewer(s) for their time and the great opportunity. This shows that you are aware of their value, and respectful of their time. Next, I would say something along the lines of, "Integrity is extremely important to me. I believe in being up front and honest with both good and bad information. So, I'd like to go ahead and tell you about a mistake I made in the past." At this point the interviewers are not judging you in any harsh way, but you have captured their full attention. This is when you should try to build the context of your crime instead of just saying you have a criminal record. I've found the C.O.D.C. story line (see below) to be extremely helpful.

C.O.D.C. Story Line

- What was your life like before the crime?
  (**Circumstances**)
- Take responsibility for the crime and punishment.
  (**Ownership**)
- What have you learned from your mistakes.
  (**Development**)
- What actions have you taken to better yourself.
  (**Change**)

Explain any circumstances that may have led to you committing the crime, such as hard times, drug addiction, depression, or even just hanging out with the wrong crowd. Although your interviewer(s) probably don't have a criminal record, most people can relate to these things in one way or another. This helps them feel closer to your circumstances, which will reduce cognitive dissonance. That's a fancy way of saying your crime won't seem as extreme if they understand where you were in life. Just make sure you're not avoiding taking the responsibility. You can think of this step as giving your interviewer(s) a baseball glove before you pitch.

Now that everyone has a glove on, they're ready to hear the rest of your story, so go ahead and throw the ball. Be sure to briefly explain your conviction, any time served, community service completed, and restitution paid. You want them to know that you have already been punished for your crime. They should also know how the punishments impacted you and your character. For instance, I always say, "My time incarcerated gave me sobriety and a clear mind for the first time in years. I quickly realize that I was headed down a path I did not want to go down. I used the time to read dozens of books and earn my G.E.D." Frame your time served or community service so that the interviewer(s) perceive you came out a better person.

Once you've explained your punishments and how they affected you, be sure to point out two or three things you are doing to turn your life around. Your family, work, school, church, community, and passions are some excellent examples of things to talk about. Do your best to relate these things to the job for which you are interviewing. A couple examples are: "Since I was arrested ten years ago, I've found love and purpose in my life. Between my wife and my dog, I get so much love and encouragement. I now understand the importance of

building a career so that I can provide for my loved ones."
Or "I love leading A.A. meetings. This has been a great
way for me to give back to my community and set a good
example for others to follow." These statements show
characteristics of good employees such as dependability
and leadership. They also give you a chance to make
yourself look good again after telling them about your
record.

An effective way to close out your story with a net
positive is to summarize <u>who you are now</u> and <u>what you
have to offer</u>. Highlight your personal mission and values
to show that your actions are built on a solid foundation.
Believe it or not, the hiring decision often comes down to
the candidate's core values and personality. Also,
remember to talk in terms of the job position you are
applying for when explaining what skills and abilities you
have to offer.

Chapter 7: **Interviewing Done Right**

To be great at interviewing is a valuable skill. Anyone who can persuade others why they are the best for the job will never be poor or unemployed. However, it often takes a lot of preparation, effort, and resilience just to get in front of a hiring manager to explain your criminal record in person. If you haven't made it this far yet, keep your determined mindset, continue networking, and put in applications. This stressful and exhausting process gets easier every time you go through it. If you have made it this far, congratulations! You are on the right track. However, explaining your criminal record in a way that keeps you in the game is only the beginning - now you must win the game. While interviewing, there are many ways to gain and lose points such as your confidence, spoken word, body language, resume, attire, and post-interview communications. Let's touch base on each topic.

Your Confidence

If you want someone to believe you are right for the job, you better believe you are right for it first. You can't say, "Umm… I think I can do that" or "I might be good at this". Whatever job or career you are pursuing, own it. Say you *can* do it and that you *are* good at it. If you have to exaggerate your ability a little to get the job, who cares. If you get the job offer, spend the next weeks studying and practicing those skills you stretched the truth about. Just don't completely lie and say you are proficient with something that you've never done. The point is, if you look, sound, and act confident, people will believe in you.

Your Words

Knowing yourself and the position you are applying for will allow you to be able to communicate without using filler words. "Umm…" is the most commonly used filler word but there are others such as "Like…" and "Well…" Some people use them when they are nervous and others do this when they are thinking. Either way, the listener will perceive this to be a negative characteristic. The greatest speakers consider their words, talk slowly and pause often. Employers want people who can express their thoughts in a clear and concise manner. The first step to cutting out filler words is to recognize that you may be overusing them. A helpful exercise is to have someone read you a behavioral-based question and count the number of times you use filler words.

Another type of word that can help you build your career is a name. Dale Carnegie wrote, "Remember that a person's name is to that person the sweetest and most important sound in any language." Try remembering and calling people by their names. It seems very simple, yet so many people, including myself, are still working to master this skill. Everyone loves to talk with the person who says, "Hey Jeff, how was your weekend?" People associate hearing their names with strong relationships such as friends and family. Saying someone's name shows that you acknowledge and care about them.

Your Body Language

Your chances of getting the job can be greatly affected by your use of body language. This form of communication can be used to your advantage no matter your education or level of experience. However, actions such as fidgeting, slouching, crossing your arms, avoiding eye contact, and bouncing your feet can cost you the job. These actions display discomfort, dishonesty, a lack of focus, and a lack of confidence. Don't bother taking notes during your interviews as many interviewers find it to be disrespectful. Definitely don't doodle! Your padfolio is only for you to take down extremely important info or for you to jot down some notes after the interview while things are fresh on your mind. When you are interviewing you should sit up straight, make eye contact often, and smile. Your body language should be making the statement that you are confident and pleasant.

Your Content

The information you communicate during the process is only as helpful as it is relevant, so the first step is to understand the position you are applying for inside and out. This will help you focus your communication on the value you can bring to the company. Typically, job postings will have a list of expectations or requirements for the position. Take time to thoroughly read the job specifications before the interview to better understand the skills the interviewers are looking for.

You should at least know the following:

1.) The company's mission and values.

2.) How they make money.

3.) What skills they are looking for.

When the interviewers ask you questions, you should be able to tie your answers back to the position which you're applying for and to the company's bigger picture mission.

Conversely, don't ask dumb questions. It is common for interviewers to ask you if you have any questions. This is not a trap; you absolutely should ask at least two or three questions. In fact, not asking questions can make it seem as if you are not all that interested in the position. They know that anyone who is truly excited about the position should have some questions. Ask open-ended questions like: Can you tell me more about the training week? How can new hires get involved with projects in your company? How does this company approach performance management?

You should avoid bringing up any negative information about the company while you are interviewing.

For instance, you would not want to bring up how today's Wall Street Journal claimed 2018 was going to be a troubling year for the auto industry if you were interviewing with Ford. Talking about a company's stock price drop, lawsuits, or unhealthy products only brings bad vibes to the conversation.

Interview Questions

The most common interviewing practice today is behavioral questioning. This means that the interviewer will ask open-ended questions like, "Tell me about a time you took initiative." Or "Tell me about a time you failed." These questions quickly expose the candidates that are either unprepared or don't have the experience required. The good news is, with preparation you can answer these questions like a professional. Most business schools teach their students to use the S.T.A.R. method which stands for Situation, Task, Action, and Results, as seen on the next page. I can't express enough the value of this simple tool in interviewing. Learn this tool like the back of your hand and it will serve you well.

S.T.A.R. Method Example

Interviewer: Tell me about a time your coworkers or manager decided to follow your advice.

You:

Situation: While I was working at the local coffee shop I noticed that we were wasting a lot of products and losing money due to employee mistakes.

Task: I decided to create a simple process to reduce waste and presented it to my coworkers and boss.

Action: I typed up a 4-point checklist that would eliminate waste if followed correctly and had it laminated. I explained to my manager the value of the checklist and she agreed.

Result: After posting the checklist for employees to follow, waste was reduced by twenty percent.

It's impossible to have a S.T.A.R. answer ready for every possible question but there are a dozen or so extremely common questions you should always be ready for. Spend some time reflecting on any past experiences you've had that relate to the position for which you are applying. Write down a few experiences for these commonly valued employee traits: Taking initiative, problem-solving, teamwork, effective communication, conflict resolution, and handling failure. Once you have identified your experiences, try to explain them using the star method. It's surprising how one experience can be used to answer several different behavior questions.

Closing the Interview

Toward the end of the interview process, the interviewer will either tell you that they have all the information they need or they will ask if you have any further questions. These are signals that it's time to finish up. There are a few notable dos and don'ts for closing the interview that you should be aware of.

You should never ask about compensation, health benefits, or vacation days during the interview. This shows a lack of focus and respect. If the interviewer decides they want to give you a second-round interview or hire you, they will either talk with you about the compensation at the end of the interview or they will send you a formal offer letter. The offer letter is usually sent via email. The final question you should ask in an interview is either: "Do you have a business card?" or "What are the next steps in the process?"

In chapter five we talked about how to tell the story of your criminal record. You should end your interview the same way you ended your story; with a net positive. This is your last chance to let them know that you are excited about the opportunity and that you are the right person for the job. Don't go over every point you made during the interview again. Simply highlight one or two of your skills along with something you would enjoy about the job that makes it right for you.

Once you have stood up, be sure to thank each interviewer for their time and consideration. This means you stand up, make eye contact, shake their hand, and say, "thank you", using their names. They will usually tell you their names at the beginning of the interview so try and remember them. I usually say a person's name in my head a few times when people tell me. Even the best minds often struggle with names so if you do forget, ask them to please tell you again. You don't want to leave without saying the interviewer's name.

Post Interview Communications

In some cases, you might find out if you got the job or not during the interview. However, the employer will often want some time to think it over or discuss it with others. You may even have to do more than one interview. During the time between your first interview and the employer making a decision, you will want to remain in contact without seeming pushy. Even after you have been hired or told that you will not be hired, you should communicate your appreciation.

If you don't receive a call or email from the company which you interviewed within three days, send a follow up email. Unless, of course, they told you it would take longer. You can see an example of a post interview email on the next page.

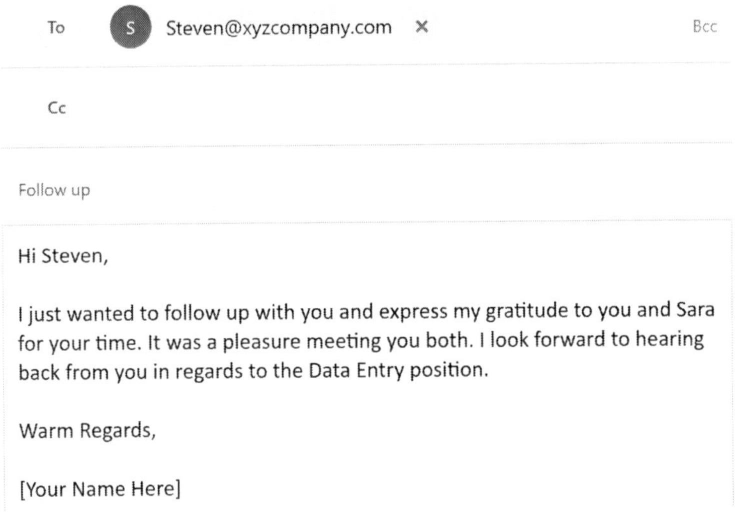

To Steven@xyzcompany.com Bcc

Cc

Follow up

Hi Steven,

I just wanted to follow up with you and express my gratitude to you and Sara for your time. It was a pleasure meeting you both. I look forward to hearing back from you in regards to the Data Entry position.

Warm Regards,

[Your Name Here]

Figure 4. Follow Up Email

In the event that you receive an email or call, explaining that you will not be getting the position, you should still respond respectfully. Whether it’s an email or phone call, you should always thank them for their time and consideration. It is also wise to express your genuine interest in the company and ask that they considered for other positions that may open in the future.

Chapter 8: **Continuous Improvement**

In Chapter Two, you read how your future level of success will be determined by the daily habits you consistently practice. Similarly, you can dramatically improve your education, income, and career by continually making smaller incremental changes. While speaking about making improvement in business processes, W. Edwards Deming once said, "It is not necessary to change. Survival is not mandatory." Whether you dropped out of high school or you have a PhD, learning new skills and knowledge should be a lifelong endeavor. Once you have a job, building your career will depend on your ability to continuously improve your value as an employee or future business owner.

Over the past few years, I've learned it to be true that luck is what happens when preparation meets opportunity. Great jobs and promotions aren't given to lucky people; they are awarded to people who are ready when the opportunity presents itself. It's unlikely that a company will approach you and say, "We will need a software engineer in 6 months. If you can take the classes and get certified, I'll hire you." You must take initiative and earn the certification first before someone will consider you for the opportunity. The important idea here is that you want to improve yourself, while knowing that better opportunities will come as a result. Always remember that you determine your own luck.

People and Environments

A large part of your success or failure can be attributed to the people you surround yourself with. Let the greatest people you know cause you to "level up", and become the best version of yourself. If you have three unemployed friends and one friend with a career, which one do you think you can learn more from? Businessman and self-help author W. Clement Stone wrote, "You are a product of your environment. So choose the environment that will best develop you toward your objective. Analyze your life in terms of its environment."

When I was released in 2012, I moved from Georgia to Ohio where I knew only a few people. Shortly after the move, I decided to go back to school at a local community college. These new environments were extremely helpful in my professional development. Your best environment may be at home, work, college, a new city, or just a quiet place to study and practice your skills.

Work Ethic

The definition of work ethic by dictionary.com is "a belief in the moral benefit and importance of work and its inherent ability to strengthen character." We have all heard the term "Learning the value of a dollar." Understanding the value of honest hard work helps you build character as well as monetary value. Your work ethic will likely develop with your age, education, and career. Here are a few things you should always be aware of and perhaps, continuously improve on.

Integrity – Be honest and have strong moral principles.

Accountability – It is your duty to do your work, take full responsibility for it.

Quality – Do your best work, not just the bare minimum.

Discipline – Commit to finishing what you start.

Teamwork – Help others and do what you said you will.

You will rarely hear of successful people with bad work ethics. However, lacking solid work ethic is a common reason companies let people go.

Reputation

Your reputation is the opinions that other people share and believe to be true about your habits and performances. A good reputation can be damaged in a matter of seconds, whereas a bad reputation takes much more time and effort to mend. Everything you say and do can affect your reputation but the things you say and do habitually will account for most of your reputation.

Take ownership and responsibility for the agreements you make with others. Whether it is a deadline for work, a time you will pick up your kid, or the number of job applications you will put in every day - <u>Make it a habit to do what you said you would do, when you said you would do it.</u>

Studies show that on average, people actually do what they said they would do, when they said they would do it about 70% of the time. To begin building a reputation as a highly reliable person, start doing what you say you are going to do, when you say you are going to do it 90-100% of the time.

People's beliefs and opinions about your habits and performances will adjust to what they see you do consistently. Building and keeping a good reputation is key to having a successful career.

Education

There is immense value in pursuing a higher level of education, even with a criminal record. The fact that you have a criminal record makes your education even more important. That is not to say that you need to take out fifty grand in student loans and get a college degree but rather you should be setting yourself apart from the crowd with valuable knowledge or skill sets.

G.E.D.

If you don't currently have a high school diploma or G.E.D., research how to earn one in your area. Most jails and prisons offer free G.E.D., programs – which you should take advantage of if you are still incarcerated. For those of you who have been released, simply search Google for G.E.D. programs in your city and sign up for the preparation courses. In Ohio, the G.E.D. exam costs $40 for first time test takers and $120 every retake. Here are a few notable reasons to get your G.E.D.:

- Employment – You will be eligible for more jobs.
- Self-Esteem – You will feel better about yourself.
- Role Model – Sets a good example for others.
- Education – Allows you to pursue higher education.

Dave Thomas, the founder of Wendy's, went back and got his G.E.D. at age 61. Although he was already an extremely successful business man, he wanted to be a better role model for younger generations. If you don't already have a diploma or G.E.D., step outside of your comfort zone and go for it.

Self-Taught

There is so much content on the internet these days that you can learn practically anything for next to nothing. Billionaire tech entrepreneur and owner of the Dallas Mavericks, Mark Cuban explained, "Where it really clicked was when I realized I could teach myself how to program in Basic, some "old school" programming languages, and could pick up any type of technology if I just spent the time to read the manual." Anyone who is resourceful and motivated can teach themselves enough to be dangerous. Most successful entrepreneurs attribute their success to their own teachings and technical obsessions rather than their traditional educations. Continuous improvement is about always learning. Reading books, watching tutorials on YouTube, and putting yourself around the right people, these are the types of changes that add up to valuable skills and knowledge.

Skilled Trades

Another type of education many people with criminal records might want to consider is learning a skilled trade. These are career skills that require specific training and often some level of higher education. Skilled trades include: Facilities Maintenance, Electrician, Welding, Plumbing, Carpentry and many others. Most skilled trades certificates can be earned in under a year and a half at your local community college. Skilled trades can earn you anywhere from $15 to $50 an hour. If you can, buy yourself the equipment needed for your trade and practice at home while working towards your certification.

If you get the certification, own some of your own equipment and you can show off some of your work, you will more than likely find a job.

Associate's or Bachelor's Degrees

College isn't for everybody; some people don't want it and others don't need it. However, in an economy of rapid technological advancement and a shrinking middle class, getting a college degree may make for the best chance of building a career. Of course, this is risky since you have a criminal record but with more risk comes more reward. If pursuing a college degree is something you're considering, you should ask yourself three questions. When answering these questions, it is critically important to be thoughtful and completely honest with yourself.

1. Have you changed?

If you're still doing the same things you were before you got arrested, then you probably shouldn't go to college. You shouldn't be using drugs (even marijuana), stealing, fighting, or partying often. Additionally, you should consider if you have something now that will make you better in school, which you didn't have before. For me this was focus. I had a hard time learning in the classroom throughout middle school due to ADHD. However, in my early twenties I became much calmer and more focused. If you're still doing the same old stuff and haven't made meaningful changes in your life, forget about college. If you were to go to college without changing, you would likely struggle to pass your classes and have a hard time finding a company that believes in you enough to hire you.

2. Can you sustain 2-5 years of college?

Earning a degree takes a long time. Many people don't pursue college degrees for precisely that reason. An associate's degree takes between 2-3 years while a bachelor's degree can take up to 5 years. Of course, the length of time it requires you to complete a degree will be determined by how many classes you take each semester and if you attend summer classes.

While working towards your degree you are almost guaranteed to run into financial issues more than once. I ran into financial issues 3 or 4 times. While attending college, you can only work so much, and when problems occur you can't just drop school. You should work enough to build yourself a safety net with no less than $3,000 before starting college. Your safety net will help you deal with unpredictable issues like your car breaking down, a child being sick, or someone stealing your laptop.

When I finally decided to go to college, I had about $1,000 a month in bills between my car, insurance, rent, and utilities. As an independent student, I was able to have about half my tuition covered with grants and scholarships. Since I was paying for the other half myself, I continued working and took out student loans. If you think you might not be able to sustain the time requirement of a college degree, *be very cautious taking out student loans*. Going thousands of dollars in debt and not finishing the degree is a place you really don't want to be. For me, taking out student loans was a great idea; I had saved a few thousand dollars, had a solid vision of what I wanted to do, and I wasn't going to take "no" for an answer.

3. Are you ready to work your ass off?

Completing a college degree can be very challenging depending on your current level of education and how long it's been since you took classes. I dropped out of high school in tenth grade and got my GED at 19. So when I started college, I was placed in the lowest available college math and writing courses, and even then I struggled at first. Are you prepared to study 2-3 hours a night instead of relaxing after a long day? Perhaps it will be even more challenging to make the leap from graduation into a career, given your criminal record. It will likely be an uphill battle painted with rejection and distress. You must try to find the lesson to be learned in every rejection, and keep trudging forward.

More college graduates are struggling to find gainful employment than ever before. However, you'll have something that the other students looking for job won't; A tough skin. Resilience. An underdog story. An impressive journey. The power to overcome tremendous adversity. An emotional investment. Fight. Grit. To pursue a degree with a criminal record is like signing up for a 2-5 year long boxing match where your "right to a better life" is the prize. Are you ready to work your ass off?

Credit

The first week after being released, my aunt told me I needed to see if I owed anyone money. When I looked into it, I discovered that I owed my old cell phone provider nearly $700. At the time, the last thing I wanted to do was pay the remaining balance from over a year earlier. However, she convinced me to do so after explaining how important it would be to my future success.

If you have any outstanding balances on a loan, cell phone, or insurance policy, you should call them and set up a payment plan. Often times they will lower the amount owed if you start making payments. I can tell you from experience that it feels great to get your debt payed off.

Once you have paid off all of your debt you should begin to build your credit. Having good credit makes life easier. Good credit will help you get approved for home, auto, and business loans faster and with lower interest rates. Talk with your bank about how you can establish credit. I also recommend visiting CreditKarma.com and set up an account to begin tracking and managing your credit score.

I hope that this chapter inspires you to continually improve your life. Remember, if you do not care about your own personal and professional development, no one else will. Whether it be your work ethic, the people you surround yourself with, your skill, or your education, you should always push yourself to do better. Small incremental achievements quickly add up to significant improvement.

Chapter 9: **Network Equals Net Worth**

A significant portion of jobs and promotions, especially higher level ones are filled by a current employee referring someone they know. With thousands of people applying for jobs daily, employers use references to make the task of hiring new people easier. At some point, you've probably heard the saying, "It's not what you know, it's who you know!" That's such a common saying because it's absolutely true, and even more so for people with criminal records.

Put simply, your network is just an informally connected group of people. This can mean family, friends, former teachers and coaches, co-workers, cellmates, people from church and anyone else you might know. You're networking every time you talk with someone while standing in line, when you get together with someone for a drink, or when you bump into an old classmate. Networking is building and maintaining relationships – any of which could provide you with useful information about a job opportunity.

The only difference between ordinary socializing and networking is the way you think about your job hunt. Instead of realizing that you don't know anyone who will hire you, networking allows you to realize that you know dozens of people who know people that may have information which could lead to a job.

Who You Should Network With

Everyone with and without criminal records should constantly be trying to create bigger and better networks. Your first thought might be that you don't know anyone to network with, but I assure you there are countless opportunities if you make a point to look for them. Below are the six primary sources you should start with while building your personal network.

1.) Family
2.) Family Friends
3.) Friends
4.) Friends of Friends
5.) Co-Workers

6.) Friends of Co-Workers

A great job opportunity could be one conversation away. Make time to call or meet in person with everyone in your network. Although they may not know of anything at the moment, they have their own network comprised of friends, family, co-workers, bosses and institutions. Ask them if they know anyone you could contact that could help you find an opportunity. Ask for an email address, phone number, or personal introduction.

How to Network

1.) Respect the other person's time.

Successful people tend to run on a tight schedule so be aware of their time constraints. Let them know why you want to meet with them and how much time you will need. You should expect that they will likely not be able to meet with you right away. You should expect them to schedule the meeting at least one week out (maybe even two or three weeks out).

It's okay to make some small talk but for the sake of time be sure to have a few specific questions for the other person. Do not be afraid to ask something like, "I am look to become a maintenance technician. Given your experience in the field, I was wondering what advice you might be able to give me. How do I get my foot in the door with a company like yours?". Although they might not be able to help you get a job with their company right then, most people like sharing their knowledge and you've created a connection that can be beneficial for many years.

2.) Listen more.

Make sure that conversations are balanced. You want to ask for their help but you also need to show interest in what they have to say. When people perceive you to be a good listener, they are more likely to help you out. As Dale Carnegie said, "You can make more friends in two months by becoming interested in other people than you can in two years by trying to get other people interested in you." People love to talk and can tell if you are truly interested in what they have to say.

3.) Seek information and advice.

It may seem odd at first to meet with someone for the purpose of finding a job and not actually ask if they know of any job openings. You have to be strategic in your approach when asking such a question. Plant the seed by seeking information about the individual's personal career or industry. Ask for advice such as, "What's the best way to get into that industry?" or "What advice would you give to someone with little experience?"

When you ask people for advice they appreciate that you trust their opinion. By showing interest in the information they give you and trusting their advice, you are planting a seed that could very well grow into them recommending you for a position at their company or sending you to a friend who could also help you find employment.

4.) Keep an information record.

In most cases, you won't get a job offer the first time you network with someone. So it's important to keep a record of their personal information so that you can follow up and reach out to them again in the future. You should take note of:

- First & Last Name.
- Their Company and Job Title.
- Email & Phone Number if possible.

- Any facts, past jobs, or people they know.

As you continue your networking and job search, you can periodically send an email sharing some information that they may be interested in such as an article or anything that made you think of them. This helps them remember that you are friends and that you may still be looking for work.

5.) Add value.

Networking is a two-way street. Typically, people help others in their network with the thought in mind that in the future they may need a favor in return. This isn't to say you should keep score because that is certainly not the case. However, you should try to make networking relationships mutually beneficial. Given your criminal record you probably won't be able to help others as much as they can help you – at first. So be aware and on the lookout for ways to provide value to the people in your network.

The goal is not to be pushy or ask for favors but rather take a sincere interest in you network contacts. The best networkers work hard to develop a relationship, establish credibility and share information. When networking, you should mostly listen and let the other person talk 50%- 80% of the time. If they stop talking, ask another question about their interests or career. You want to learn as much as you can about the people which you network, while giving them time to realize what a great listener you are.

When you learn to use other people's networks you quickly realize that you have a lot of people to network with. Find out who your coworkers know, who your relatives know, and who your neighbors know. If someone says that they have a relative who is the manager of a company, you should ask some more questions and see if you can get their contact information. Just make sure that you get permission to reach out to the contact before doing so. Wherever you are, be aware that you may be one connection away from a better career and life.

Where to Network

EVERYWHERE. Once of my friends, was working in the kitchen of a hospital making low wages. None of her coworkers were executives or corporate managers but she networked with them nonetheless. She told her co-workers she was looking to leave the hospital to try and start a career in Human Resources. One of her co-workers said that her longtime neighbor was an H.R. executive at Cardinal Health and that she would put in a good word. A few weeks later she received a call to set up an interview. It doesn't matter who you are around, if you network effectively, people will vouch for you and opportunities will arise.

The highest paying job I had before graduating college was working as a data entry clerk for a small retail consulting firm in Westerville, Ohio. I had no experience in the industry and was underqualified when I was hired for the position. I landed this job purely through networking.

I never expected that going to my grandmother's Halloween party would pay off so well but it did. While I was playing with my little cousins, my grandmother introduced me to one of her lifelong friends. She told me that he was an entrepreneur in Columbus. After asking him a few questions I discovered that he had gotten his MBA from Harvard Business School and had quite a successful career. I asked him about his business, how he got into the industry, and if he enjoyed working for himself.

Before leaving he gave me a business card and said I could email him if I ever had any questions. I sent him a few emails here and there asking questions and giving him updates on my interests and job search. It wasn't until nearly a year later that he emailed me asking if I was interested in working for his company. He once told me that "Your net worth is in your network". He is a highly respected man who has mastered the art of networking with big companies, as well as little people like me. You never know when you'll meet someone like this.

LinkedIn

LinkedIn is a business and employment-related social networking website. People rarely handout business cards these days while they are networking. It's now more common in professional setting for people to connect on LinkedIn. Creating a profile allows you to easily connect with friends, co-workers, professors, and anyone else you'd like to network with. I use LinkedIn daily and it has been incredibly helpful throughout my career, especially when building my business and my personal brand.

Finding Mentors

Successful people have mentors. Bill Gates credits much of his success to his mentor, Warren Buffet, who credits his success to Benjamin Graham. Mark Zuckerberg was mentored by Steve Jobs and Jobs was mentored by Andy Grove. I was mentored by two men that I highly respect. Whether it's your basketball coach, your boss at work, or a business executive you met through a family member, you should try and find a mentor and meet at least once a month. Oprah Winfrey described mentors as, "Someone who allows you to see the hope inside yourself."

While networking, you will likely find a person or two you seem to click with. They may have been through similar experiences or perhaps they think you are very intelligent. Either way, this is likely a relationship that could become more of a mentor/mentee situation. You should thank everyone who takes the time to network with you, but take an extra step for the exceptional few by letting them know you enjoyed meeting with them and would like to meet with them again in the future.

Mentors are like advisors that help you develop as a person and in your career. They are usually older and more experienced than their mentees, bringing valuable wisdom to the relationship. This type of relationship fosters more open and in-depth discussions. Typically, you can talk to your mentor about your failures and struggles where as you wouldn't in ordinary networking relationships. As Denzel Washington testified, "Show me a successful individual and I'll show you someone who had real positive influences in his or her life. I don't care what you do for a living—if you do it well I'm sure there was someone cheering you on or showing the way. A mentor."

Whether you're looking to start a career or you're retired, both networking and mentorship are rewarding and valuable. Meet as many people as you can, seek advice, listen with interest, give and receive helpful information, and build lasting relationships. That is the essence of networking and mentorship.

Chapter 10: **Your Life Story**

The idea to write this book came while I was considering the best advice I could give to a group of men in prison faced with the challenge of finding jobs once they were released. At that moment, it hit me that any quick piece of advice would be inadequate. My hope is that you will be able to secure a job after reading this book, but that will just be the beginning of your journey. Every individual that reads this book is facing different circumstances. You will still have to travel your own journey and experience your own trials and triumphs. However, recidivism statistics mean nothing when you decide to take control of your life.

When I began writing this book, I realized that my struggle with incarceration and living with a criminal record was more than something to overcome. It was part of my life story and something to build on. I had crossed a critical point where I could speak of my criminal record as a pro instead of a con. Explaining my past began speaking more to my strengths than my weaknesses. I believe this critical point exists for everyone with a criminal record. With the right attitude and a commitment to self-improvement, you can turn your past into an asset that actually helps you.

Underdog

Coming straight out of jail or prison you won't be viewed as an underdog. However, you can earn that title fairly quickly by exceeding people's expectations through thoughtful and consistent action. Psychology research shows that most people feel a deep connection to underdogs. As one article described it:

"We tend to evaluate underdogs in a positive light. Some researchers believe this might have something to do with deeply held beliefs of justice and fairness. Fairness is one of the most frequently endorsed character strengths around the world. There are seeds of fairness in every person. By definition, the underdog does not fare as well as the top dog thus it is easy for a fan's fairness buttons to be pushed where they root for the underdog to have a chance to make it to the limelight."

"In order to win, underdogs must express a high degree of effort. And they express this effort over a long duration, surpassing the obstacles that come their way. This describes the character strength of perseverance. Perseverance is one of the most motivating character strengths to view." (Psychcentral - The Psychology of the Underdog)

Maintaining a job should be your number one priority, then building a fulfilling career. As you develop better skills and learn new knowledge you'll be able to reflect on how far you've clearly come. Others will begin to see you as an underdog because you will have likely exceeded their expectations.

Know that when people see you as an underdog they'll typically want to see you succeed. Interviewers are no different. Many of the people who interview you will want to help you. Whether they do or not will depend on if they can make that call on their own, the relationship they have with their boss, and the company's policies. If you're persistent with your job search and networking, you'll find someone who perceives you to be an underdog and can influence the final decision of you receiving a job offer.

Living for a Legacy

A clinical professor and former vice president of a multi-billion-dollar heath care company taught me the power of identifying what you want your personal legacy to be. The career you peruse, the money you earn, and the car you drive will mean nothing once you are gone. People will remember you as a loving parent or a busy parent, for your joy or your stress, your greed or your generosity, your values or your motives. The idea was not to be selfless but to be aware of the legacy you will leave while you're still around to craft it. What words do you think people associate with you? Whenever you are dead and gone, how will people remember you?

The fact that you've had trouble with the law doesn't mean that you'll necessarily be thought of and remembered as a bad or troubled person. Many highly admired people came from rough backgrounds such as crime, abuse, and poverty. People with the longest journeys never forgot where they came from – they're often more generous and humble than the more fortunate.

There are countless examples of people with troubled pasts doing amazing things. In Bill George's book

"Discover Your True North" he explains, "Most of the leaders we interviewed were shaped by severe trials in their lives, which we call crucibles. Psychologist Abraham Maslow found that tragedy and trauma were the most important human learning experiences leading to self-actualization."

Howard Schultz, CEO and Chairman of Starbucks Coffee Company, was born in a Brooklyn, N.Y. and lived in a government housing project. He now has a net worth of $1.5 billion. Mr. Schultz makes sure that his employees get the best work benefits including: bonuses, 401(k) matching, free college, and discounted stock purchase options for everyone working 20 hours a week or more. His company also offers full tuition reimbursement to employees who want to seek a college degree.

As a BestFriends.org article describes, "Danny Trejo is one of Hollywood's most recognizable character actors, yet his road to success has been hard earned. He grew up on the streets of Los Angeles, and despite spending the latter part of his youth and early adulthood incarcerated, he has risen to become a great actor and better person. Upon his release from Salinas Valley State Prison,

Danny became involved in programs aimed at helping those who, like him, battled or are battling drug and alcohol addictions. He is also a devoted animal lover and animal advocate with five adopted rescue dogs of his own."

Take the time to write a personal legacy statement. Try to sum up what you want to accomplish in your life and how you want be remembered in one long sentence. You can think of it like you are writing your own eulogy. This might take you five minutes or five weeks. I've found that writing and reflecting on a legacy statement reduces stress and anxiety, motivates action, and raises self-esteem. It's easy for us to get over-invested in our pursuit of success and forget what's most important.

Sharing Your Story

The way you talk and share your story will develop and evolve with your experiences, values, failures, and successes. Early in your life with a criminal record, sharing your story will help you find people who can relate to you, understand the struggle you're going through and possibly help you. Later in your life, once you have begun to overcome tremendous obstacles, you will share your story for other reasons. You have the potential to influence young people, to mentor others, and to change the culture of your community. When we unlock our potential to help others, the world becomes a much better place to live.

As the hip-hop artist Murs said, "I'm just a dude who tries to do right. You know I try to make my tomorrows better than my yesterdays without hurting anyone else in the process. Cause if you leave the world a better place than it was when you got here, then we all win."

Over the past few years I found it incredibly challenging to get a job and build a career with a criminal record. Even though I don't have all the answers, I do know that the topics I wrote about in this book are what helped me find my own success.

I will consider this book a success if it helps even one person have a better life. American author Louis L'Amour once said, "Knowledge is like money: to be of value it must circulate, and in circulating it can increase in quantity and, hopefully, in value." Please, share this book with someone else who may benefit from reading it. – Thank You.

References:

Introduction:

Durose, M. R., Cooper, A. D., Ph.D., & Snyder, H. N., Ph.D. (2014). Recidivism of Prisoners Release in 30 States in 2005: Patterns from 2005 to 2010. 1-31. Retrieved January 2017.

Your Life:

The Psychology of the Underdog. (n.d.). Retrieved January 11, 2017, from https://blogs.psychcentral.com/character-strengths/2012/03/the-psychology-of-the-underdog/

Living a Legacy:

Danny Trejo. (2015, August 14). Retrieved February 22, 2017, from http://bestfriends.org/about/our-partners/celebrity-supporters/danny-trejo

[Recorded by N. Carter]. (2008). *Everything*. LT Moe. Retrieved March 3, 2017.

Acknowledgments:

Thank you: Patsy Gardner, Tara and Earl Rahm, Renee and Chris Ayers, Steven and Tina Scott, Steve and Nancy Morris, Yasmin Jimenez, Pam Lajoie, Lisa Newman and Lynn Belote.

Made in United States
North Haven, CT
23 January 2024